Bounce
Back
Higher

Gift Editions and Quantity Orders

This book was designed for gift giving, and can be purchased with special pricing for quantity orders. A hardcover edition, imprinted with "Special Gift Edition" and customized editions are also available.

Videos

Videos mentioned in the text may be viewed at jimlord.org/bounce-back-higher.

Community and complimentary book

Join a community and receive updates on this book and a complimentary copy and audiobook of its companion volume, *What Kind of World Do You Want?* at jimlord.org/what-kind-of-world.

For more information

For information, please send an email to quest@jimlord.org.

Second Edition ISBN 978-1-09836-653-7

Published by Serving Society, Cleveland, Ohio USA

A Note to *You* – Break the Rules

Write in the margins.

Everything in this book is offered to stimulate your thinking.

As you turn the pages of this slim volume, allow your experience to be foremost. So, write your insights in this book or in notes on your ereader or tablet.

Really.

Most of us hear the grade-school librarian in the back of our heads and treat a book as a sacred object. To that I say: Go ahead, write in this book! Make friends with it. Make it more of a conversation.

Make the book yours.

With its four 30-second questions, you may find this tiny book will not only prompt wise action today, but serve as a handy journal and memoir for you of these unusual days.

Contents

Introduction: Go Higher

AT A TIME WHEN SO MANY PEOPLE are feeling powerless, let me be bold and get right to the point: I know you have personal power. If you're looking at this book, I *know* you have given a lot and want to give even more here and now.

In my work with leaders across the US and the Americas and from Africa to Australia, I have seen so many people discover they have what it takes and the commitment to the common good to create change in the world for the better — even (especially) in dire times.

Sure, when we try to rouse ourselves to action in a dauntingly stormy era to make an inspiring and important difference, we can feel we're thwarted by headwinds. But we can also find tailwinds — strengths, inspiration, camaraderie, answers — that can propel us forward and foster change we seek. This book offers you a practical guide to finding and harnessing those tailwinds.

Think of *Bounce Back Higher* as a pathfinder and companion where you'll discover three simple but significant steps on the journey of any meaningful change or challenge — Get Out of the River; Take a Walk Along the River's Edge; and Bounce Back Higher.

Along the way, you'll encounter stories of many inspiring people (and links to short videos with them) whose experiences burn more brightly the love of humanity that lies behind the word *philanthropy*, that is, the love of humankind.

You'll find here practices and precepts developed over my fifty years of work with leaders, refined by the events of recent times and inspired by the example of philanthropists who have given and raised billions for the causes they value—and who teach us more about human motivation than any course, book, or expert I've encountered.

Come join me.

Meet some friends of mine.

Take a walk with us.

Go higher.

Lift your gaze together with the people around you.

Imagine if all the people who want to change the world *knew* they could. The time is right. In the hardest, darkest times and in spite of—or because of —our worries and challenges, we have the clarity that calls us to action like never before.

You might be one of us already, and this book will convince you that you already have all the personal power it takes.

When the Sky Is Falling, Can We Choose a Future?

You and I are enduring a pandemic, economic catastrophe, cyber-attacks, desperation, and despair. Equality denied has brought outraged people to the streets. Some have carried signs; others have carried guns.

"I can't breathe" is the cry of Eric Garner, George Floyd and a rallying cry of Black Lives Matter and victims of police violence. COVID-19 has left its victims gasping, West Coast megafires deoxygenate life. People are suffocated by stacks of bills they can't pay. It feels like an abundance of scarcity. And a crisis of trust.

And if all of that isn't enough, we are living with the breathtaking consequences of climate calamities. For the first time in human history, we know it's all connected. The sky does seem to be falling.

But who's there to put it back up? When we most need a strong democracy, we found ourselves with a stifling authoritarian rule in the name of liberty, fair elections threatened, and democracy itself at long-term risk.

While we're at it, what solace is there in the reduction of mass shootings when it's not due to government leadership, but because schools have been closed and mass gatherings discouraged, if not outlawed?

The inventory of the empty shelves of our lives goes on and on. Crises and conflict may change how they manifest, but one reality is clear: we will long be living in a time of uncertainty, trying to make sense of it all. Who knows what will arrive next?

Seems it's time to take a deep breath. (I'm serious: do it right now.) You know it, you feel it, the fraught times we confront. You're living it, even though for self-preservation, we all often mute the anguish and fear. I certainly do every day.

We're bored, listless, and unfocused. Or we're overworked and overwhelmed. Or both. It's natural to feel constricted, uncertain, and anxious these days.

Together, these paradoxical feelings make up the ancient Greek emotion of *acedia* (uh-**see**-dee-uh).

Jonathan Zecher of Australian Catholic University has revived the word used by 5th century monks living in isolation, suggesting that by naming it and saying, "I'm feeling acedia," we gain agency over the quandary.

Can We Actually Choose?

With good reason, many of us wonder, *Can we choose to create the future we most desire, or are we at the mercy of forces beyond our control?* How dare I even ask the question?

If ever there were a time to step back, pause, and figure out how each of us can best use this unsettled time as an opportunity to reframe the problems into possibilities, that time is now.

It's our time to get ready for the cascade of unexpected changes that are on their way.

Come along with me and we'll get out of the river, take a walk together, and end up being able to bounce higher, not just back to where we were. That's a heroic journey if ever there were one. We'll discover hidden leadership that can be forged only in time of crisis. We'll find resources overlooked and discounted; we will inspire the contributions—ones that people yearn to make—in ways like never before. That's the promise of these few pages and stories.

We'll meet ordinary folks who have become extraordinary in uncertain times. Like you, all of them strive to lead in their community and society, in their circle of friends and family—and in organizations that are the primary vehicles for their efforts to foster the kind of world they want.

As my point of reference, I will draw here on the work I began long ago in the vineyards of philanthropy. I was taught by the actions of civic leaders and philanthropists who practice the wonderfully odd behavior of "giving away" their money and time.

The insights I've gained apply to the breadth of humanity, all of us contributors in our own right, from the soup kitchen volunteer to those who are the beneficiaries of those sustaining meals and want just as much to make their contribution. In fact, the insights apply just the same to each and every one of us as we strive to make a difference with our lives and be contributors to society — even as "merely" a family member.

In these pandemic days, as so many invest themselves in the common good, it's painful and yet inspiring to see how people are meeting the moment, like our daughter who bravely goes to her chosen work in emergency medicine. All of us are recognizing as contributions the work others do for us in such things as stocking grocery shelves or serving us at checkout counters — actions we largely took for granted but now call "essential services."

I have wrestled to find out for myself how we can make sense of this moment. I'm going to share what I've learned in the course of my study and reflecting on my work with hundreds of leaders, many of whom would deflect the idea that they are leaders.

Together we will work through where we find ourselves and move to a new place of greater capability and contribution. It may be trite, but always behind the clouds, the sun shines brightly.

In the past, dire times have led to changes that have bent the arc of history. If the Black Death in medieval days ushered in the era of the Renaissance and then the Enlightenment, could now be our turning point to redefine what it means to be human? Shakespeare and Newton reached peaks of creativity during plagues — even as we know we are worthy without reaching those once-in-a-century kinds of peaks. I know it can sound daunting, but such a rethink can begin simply with you and me, and with small acts.

As you think about what you can rise to contribute next, you'll discover a *reframe* — a way to restore confidence, inspire people to be brave and act with renewed conviction to change the world and create the future we most desire. It's easier than it first appears. But it requires going beyond good old positive thinking and simple optimism.

In these pages, you'll find five key insights that will help you reframe how we have thought things get done and civilization advances.

- ☐ Instead of seeing only needs, we see *resources*.
- ☐ Instead of decrying our deficits, we *appreciate our assets*.
- ☐ Instead of hearing our own echoing voice in our isolation, we convene *conversations*.
- ☐ Instead of feeling hateful, we seek to *understand*.
- ☐ Instead of bouncing back, we *bounce back higher*.

But before we begin our adventure, we want to see the opportunity in this very moment — and how today we can begin our reframe, one word at a time.

Change a Word, Change a Reality

Changing a single word has the power to change your reality. It did for me at a time much like the traumatic one we are in now. We have a lot we can learn from the day that our sense of who we are as Americans and our place in the world was shattered: the cataclysmic ambush of September 11, 2001. Barely a week after that scary and raw day, I got on an airplane and braved the skies to convene a global group for a strategic retreat at the University of British Columbia.

(Like this one, most of the vignettes you'll find here and in the book, *What Kind of World Do You Want?*, come from folks who have taken part in The Philanthropic Quest™ Strategic Retreats.)

We puzzled over some unconventional ideas and improbable questions and tried to have some fun.

What if aliens, arriving on this planet, had special eyes that could perceive only our beauty, strengths, assets, blessings — the tailwinds that carry us along and that we humans often overlook or take for granted?

Such a focus is so rare, the question seeming to come out of the blue, that the replies began with painful slowness. We wrote them down on a long sheet of paper at the front of the room, leaving a little space at the top.

After we had filled the sheet, I asked the group, "What is it that we're working toward? After all is said and done, what kind of world is it that we want? What kind of world do *you* want? Can you express it in a single word, or maybe two?"

I'd asked these questions of groups many times before. That afternoon it was different. I spoke with a lump in my throat. The words came out softly, from a very deep place.

The first person to answer said she wanted a "safe" world. Heads nodded. We could all relate to that wish. In fact, I have a hunch that on that particular day, most would have called safety an urgent need. I wrote *safe* at the top of the very long sheet of paper on the wall.

Only seconds passed and Virginia Henderson, a civic leader in Australia, offered another view. "I think it's a different world than *safe*," she said. "I think that's past. It's a *confident* world I want."

With that single word, Virginia shifted our attention. Before she spoke, we had been focused on our despair, our fear, our hunger for security, and the apparently insoluble problem of terrorism. Under the circumstances, it seemed unthinkable to speak of anything else.

Virginia's wish for a *confident* world brought our inner resources to the fore and opened the possibility that we might face the future with courage and strength.

I wrote *confident* next to *safe*.

We worked with other responses for a few minutes more. Then, as we looked at all of the tailwinds propelling us, which we had listed on that same long sheet of paper at the workshop's outset, I posed a question that I always ask: "Look at the words at the top of the sheet that lay out the qualities of the kind of world we want. Can we see here any evidence among our tailwinds — any sign that at least some of what we want is already here?"

The group had gravitated toward the notion of a *confident* world, so I picked up on that and asked, "Is there any evidence that you can see of a *confident* world?"

Silence.

All of us, eyes moist, turned to look at Virginia, who had *flown* halfway around the world from Australia.

Getting from *Me* Courage to *We* Citizenry

Virginia offers us the power of vocabulary that we can use some twenty years later to perceive our trying times in the larger context of who we are as humans and leaders, identities that can eclipse the specifics of our current circumstances.

But Virginia and all of us were together in the same room. We came together as a group in our grief and resolve, trying to figure out how to navigate a new era. Instead, today, we each do the work alone, isolated, separated, and estranged from each other.

However, if we are contributors who give of ourselves, and we wear our hearts on our sleeves and our masks on our faces as symbols that we are all in this together, that common awareness transcends our physical distance and connects us in a way we wouldn't see if not for the separation forced upon us.

This time teaches us something new about what it means to be human and moves us forward as leaders who crave to make a difference. It suggests how we can relate to each other, contribute to each other, and engender a common good. It is summoning us as individuals to come together as a *we citizenry*.

In March 2020, I was preparing for a retreat at a university thousands of miles away from my home, unaware that we were headed for mortal danger and a global lockdown. I had enjoyed a brief interview with each board and staff member I would work with. I was excited, they were excited, and lots was at stake.

With the coronavirus already commanding our attention, I was taking the same posture about this retreat as I had the week after 9/11: this was a time for courage. I believed I would survive this crisis, too.

Then it suddenly dawned on me: *This is different.* There is a social responsibility to the equation, a moral imperative. Being on an airplane after 9/11 was a show of confidence. Being on a plane in the COVID-19 era could be perceived by many as a show of disrespect and irresponsibility. My epiphany was a profound lesson: *my* bravery in contrast to *our* civic responsibility.

This was one of many shifts from *me* to *we* that I have often made, now more poignant than ever, and more often since Spring 2020. Never before have I known so clearly that my actions can save or kill another.

I was trying to do what psychologists call maintaining the *normative bias*. I tried to act as if times were normal, dampening the acute awareness that was emerging—a natural reaction to a time we were all uncertain and scared. After all, simply functioning seemed more important than actually feeling what was happening. In such times, we try to dull our senses and act as if it's all okay, while at a primal level, we know it isn't.

So, How Is It Going for You, Really?

As someone who contributes through your leadership, you've developed your presence to influence others in many ways as you've faced the unknown since Spring 2020. As well, you likely end up getting in your own way at times, just as I have. We're both apt to fall into self-talk that goes something like this: "What's the matter with me? What's wrong with me?"

Kim Scott, President of Trillium Family Services, based in Portland, Oregon, and a global leader in the destigmatization movement in behavioral health, says that typical question, defaulting as it does to the presumption of dysfunction, is being replaced with a more accurate and compassionate lens that asks, "What happened to you?" Instead of pointing a finger at the individual, the focus is on the circumstances that led to the behavior that may be making life a tough road.

At a recent retreat, as we explored the question, "What could be possible for the world—and you?" Kim had a breakthrough: he realized the third question in that series could be "What is *possible* for you?" He was asking that question at the levels of the individual, family, community.

Can we now allow ourselves to embrace the promise of possibilities?

We're not alone. Others have pointed the way for us and adopted at the same time modest but transformative attitudes that can benefit you just the same. You will hear a few profound voices here. First, you can see and listen to Kim Scott talking about the three questions on the day he had his insight. It took place when he had stepped out of the river of life to reflect and talk with a group of newfound friends.

Kim Scott: jimlord.org/bounce-kim

Just How Important Is the Question of *How Are We Doing?*

It takes little imagination to see the link between forced isolation, the anxiety of crisis — and depression. Lack of physical contact and worry withers the soul. Well-documented, too, is the link between mental health and physical health. Depression, for one, is correlated with heart disease and cancer.

In one of the world's most desirable locales, Eagle River Valley, around Vail, Colorado, more suicides were reported than COVID-19 deaths in the pandemic's opening months. (In fact, leaders at Vail Health had begun a campaign to respond in the year before the pandemic.)

These deaths of despair — mostly self-inflicted deaths due to suicides, drug overdoses, and alcoholic liver disease — have taken place amid a rising tide of mental and behavioral illnesses, greater in some demographics and geographics.

Angus Deaton, the Nobel laureate who co-authored with Anne Case *Deaths of Despair*, found that their frequency was greatest among middle-aged whites. Death rates had been declining since the 1990's by 40 percent for college graduates; they are now on the rise. For those without a college degree, they rose by

25 percent. (Political philosopher Michael Sandel, who will be a major voice as we look at those who feel unheard in society, has observed that Donald Trump, now twice impeached, had the best results during the Republican primaries of 2016 in places with the highest rates of deaths of despair.)

As the saying goes, that which does not kill us makes us stronger—and that strength allows us to make a greater contribution than could have been possible before, and just as importantly, to see the significance of the contributions we've already made.

Contribution is *connection*— human relatedness that promotes health in the face of individual isolation.

The Power of Contribution in Our Lives

When we speak here of contribution, it is in the broadest sense — the abiding desire to make a difference that lives in each of us. We yearn to connect and give in common with others in a form of *tribute*.

It's a universal that applies to the beneficiaries of philanthropy and benefactors alike. The contributory spirit extends far beyond that traditional realm of good works. It animates every one of us in our daily work.

In all of these settings, people want to be a part of something beyond themselves. Contribution is how we say, even subtly or silently, "I'm here, I matter." We usually think of contribution as giving money. It's actually much broader than that, as we are learning in this pandemic. Still, looking at why people give money can help us see the mental and behavioral health benefits of prosocial behavior.

Like you, I have been grappling with daunting life questions, which have become more vivid, visceral, timely and poignant since the arrival of the pandemic. More than ever, I want to know what makes people tick, why they do what they do.

My quest for answers began fifty years ago when I started working with philanthropists and civic leaders. I wanted to understand something about the human motivation to "give away" money and devote time without personal gain.

Ever since, I've been seeking the idiosyncratic answer—one that even the contributor doesn't know in its fullness. That lifelong inquiry has taught me more about human motivation than all the books, courses, and experts I've encountered.

Consider one wealthy, generous woman who has given tens of millions of dollars to promote social justice and other causes. She's recognized as a leader who's inspired many others, including those on the ground who work day-in and day-out to make their own kind of contributions to humanity. She's a warm and deeply kind person.

"When you look back at all of the contributions you've made, which one stands out?" I asked her. "Which is most significant, most meaningful for you?"

"I really haven't done that much," she said, pausing in petting her cocker spaniel and leading me outside to fill a bird feeder.

Haven't done that much? I thought, tempted to shake her by her shoulders.

She may have noted my surprise. Scrunching up her face, she said, "Well, there are just so many needs out there, aren't there?"

As politely as I could manage, I said, "Yes, *and* there are also so many people like you who want to contribute, who want to make a difference, and I'd rather focus on your desires than on what the world needs. You inspire me to do more."

Her eyes sparkled for a moment before she looked down. I've seen the same toe-in-the-carpet self-effacement in other folks who've devoted their lives to making a difference in people's lives by working in social good organizations. Yes, their contributions eclipse the financial philanthropy that we value as paramount.

Getting people to accept this self-appreciative way of viewing our desire to give is paradoxically the way to evoke and activate the kind of contributions the world is calling for these days. These new ways are backed up by teams of researchers in the social sciences who've uncovered evidence that we go further and faster when we accept the power of what we have done instead of being weighed down by what we haven't. We get more juice when we own up to being the kind of people we are instead of being overwhelmed by the kind of problems we see.

Acknowledging what we bring, uncomfortable as that is to own up to — *that* is the work. The purpose and the power of our impact makes it worth the discomfort. We show up differently, more inspiring yet humble.

For me, some of the most inspiring examples of contributors owning their value and yet remaining grounded in their humility are found among the folks who facilitate Quest retreats, like Delanna Starks, who attended her first retreat as a college freshman.

I am in awe of how she has counseled hundreds of girls through a volunteer cause she founded, "I Am She." Watch her as she tells us, "I am the person I needed—to help people realize their worth."

Delanna Starks: jimlord.org/bounce-delanna

Delanna was thrust out of the river of life and into uncertainty many times before the pandemic struck. (She would never suggest it, but her life story reminds me how fortunate and lucky I've been.)

Thinking back to when we were all interrupted in March 2020, some sensed a great change ahead; for most of us, the dawning was gradual. Then, whether out of necessity or that normative bias, most of us jumped back into life with hardly a break to truly reflect, awkwardly balancing one foot in the river and one foot out.

Now you may have given yourself a mini-sabbatical to reorient. In any case, give yourself credit right now for at least getting out of the river long enough to take in these words.

In the next part of this little book, we'll explore three steps that move from a natural *woe is me* and *woe are we,* to something better—three steps that can lead us to greater grounding and then buoyancy so we can bring more significance to our contributions.

We'll extricate ourselves from the *river*, embark on a *pilgrim's journey*, and find ourselves able to *bounce higher*, not merely bounce back.

3 Steps
from Contemplation
to Conversation to
Inspiration

Step 1.
Get Out of the River

THESE DAYS CAN BE LONELY. How can we manage to get through them without feeling all alone and lost? One way is to feel the presence of others. As I was writing this, I experienced in the room with me people like Virginia and others you'll meet in this piece.

I also felt them with me when we all stepped out of the roiling river of life, to one degree or another, back in Spring 2020. Virginia and these fellow travelers showed up at my riverbank. In their presence, I used our unexpected interruption to reflect.

What to Do in the Face of an Existential Threat

Let me first set the context for getting out of the river.

A few days into the shutdown, I was having one of my regular conversations with one of these fellow travelers — philosopher and public elder Jay Hughes. Jay is author of *Family Wealth* and has long been a prominent adviser in the wealth-management field. (We first met at one of my programs a few years back, and he has since become my teacher.)

He pointed out something that has an uncanny connection to the threats we face now. In his book *Family Trusts,* Jay speaks of the arrival of an inheritance and how, when that gift is received, it's as if a meteor hit the person's life: "I've asked countless audiences of people who've received inheritances, 'Was it a blessing or burden?' The hands go up, evenly split."

Indeed, we are clear on the burden posed by the pandemic and the other events we face, ranging from racism and sexism to classism and climate change. But how can we make each of these existential events more of a blessing than a burden?

We do that by getting out of the river. Jay suggested this idea to me, inspired by Arnold van Gennep, author of *The Rites of Passage.* Jay delineates three stages of a successful response to an existential event. First, the river in which we're swimming is disrupted. Second, we get out of the flow, and take a contemplative break on the riverbank. Third, we get back into the water, which is now a different river, just as we are different people.

Often, such as right now, extrication from the river is thrust upon us, this time by a viral bug 1/900th the width of a human hair. It has brought humanity into an unknown world; one where long-time issues of injustice and inequality add rapids to the river — and our feelings are a significant part of this equation.

Allow me to explain why I believe this to be true. My self-revelation may be useful to you. For decades I worked at the edge of burnout at 80-90 hours a week. My mood and productivity depressed at times. My body was compromised to the point that back pain once put me in a wheelchair for a weekend.

When my intense workstyle actually paid off, there was elation and more energy, and my vision burned brightly. But when those high points subsided, I'd move into lower energy times, the vision dimming. Often I kept trudging along, as if all were fine. But other times, I found myself thrust out of the river of life, burned out.

I didn't like those periods, which some would call depression. Only later in life did I realize the upside of those quiet times: they allowed me to relax and let the fields lie fallow, knowing the land would be restored and new seeds would germinate.

I would call my experience "bipolar" if I didn't eschew the overuse of medical pathology in the everyday world, where we pathologize various *differences* in behavioral health. As Soren Kierkegaard said, "Once you label me you negate me."

I say bipolar because when I made a commitment to better understand myself, I visited a therapist, who said he would submit for insurance a diagnosis of mild bipolar. He told me that he didn't see in me the grandiosity part of the equation. I think he missed the mark on that one. After all, I'm a guy who writes a book called *What Kind of World Do You Want?*

If you have yet to take that pause to get out of the river, spending a few moments with these words can be an oasis until you can truly withdraw and step back.

Immediately jumping back into the flow without pausing forfeits the opportunity to grow for the better. If you really want to take advantage of the pause, you may want to consider one of the questions that Virginia and the group in Vancouver pondered: *What kind of world do you want? And what kind of contribution do you want to make to realizing that world?*

I'm lucky to be able even to suggest we take a pause. Too many people, caught up in our current upheaval and serving as "essential workers," have been unable to stop and rest. They have suffered so much and felt powerless and helpless to extricate themselves from the raging river. As a worker, a person striving to keep a business afloat, or as someone caring for an at-risk relative or a child who cannot return to school, that may be your experience. Whether physician or meatpacker, family member or necessary friend, many of us find no time or energy for ourselves as we struggle to save others or keep our lives intact. Whether we are overworked or unemployed or just plain scared, in 2020 all of us took on a new job of vigilance—worry, depression, anxiety, or worse.

Or you may be more like me in my good fortune and yet tell yourself that you're too busy to get out of the river.

But even if you feel too desperate or too busy, would you be open to considering a small step? Find one task, habit, or idea that can be put on a "not to-do list" and make space in your life for something new?

If we can give ourselves some time and space to pause, we gain perspective and see a fresh path forward, to move from contemplating to exploring as we walk beside the river to see what we can find.

Am I making sense to you? Is it a worthy idea?

Ask Yourself...
(30-Second Question #1)

Are you open to considering the notion of getting out of the river and taking a mini-sabbatical — for just a few days, a few hours?

(Or will you use this little book as your time out of the river right now?)

Sometimes it's only a matter of giving ourselves permission to take care of ourselves.

Step 2.
Take a Walk Along the River's Edge

As I SAT ON THE RIVERBANK, I realized I had been on a pilgrim's journey ever since I was with Virginia and the group just after 9/11, seeking the *confident* world she wanted for us.

Today, restoring a new version of confidence and conviction seems even more elusive than it was in 2001. Might this question be worth your considering: What would make more sense than to walk together along the river, traversing a terrain new to all of us — people of different classes and walks of life from the world over — and telling each other stories?

Jay Hughes illuminated the idea by recalling *The Canterbury Tales*. In that epic tale, written during the Black Plague, Chaucer tells us each of his characters were on their own lonely journeys, thrown together by chance. Jay recounts the innkeeper saying to the travelers, "It's less lonely on your pilgrimage if you tell others your stories."

When I got out of the river, I sat on the riverbank to make sense of what was going on, and then roused myself to the pilgrim's journey, walking and talking along the riverbank, knowing the trek was more important than the destination.

As you set out for Ithaka,
hope the voyage is a long one,
full of adventure, full of discovery.
—C.P. Cavafy

In the first weeks of my journey, at Whole Foods, I saw Maurice who would always offer me a taste of his favorite produce in his section. His work helped me see more clearly than ever the vital jobs performed by people we didn't know were essential. Those who stock the shelves in the grocery store. Those who deliver the food. Those who grow the food. Those who cook and clean and protect and maintain. Many of them have only basic formal education, earn little pay—and receive little status until we became fearful for the first time that we could run out of food to eat.

Michael Sandel points out, "It is hard to resist the tendency to confuse the money we make with the value of our contribution to the common good."

In tiny human moments like these, the life-giving power is not the new landscapes that appear, but familiar ones seen with new eyes.

When we were shocked by the pandemic's arrival, all of us turned to whatever help and guidance we could find. Through these dire days, Elisabeth Kübler-Ross's stages of grief have applied equally to the pandemic, but with one addition: a phase after acceptance— making meaning. Her co-author, David Kessler, says, "In this dark time, people are finding meaning through connection and are realizing they are not as remote from each other as they thought."

On this journey of yours, you can use the stories here (and in the post-9/11 book you'll be able to access) to find a springboard for your own meaning-making—and to envision where you're going, or better yet, where you want to go, and the inspiration to get there.

A New Way to
View a New Time

Along our path, we realize whatever our losses, what is durable and endures is this truth: *Unexpected tough times have arisen and will again. Our indefatigable human spirit asks us to look back at terrible times and find value in the struggle and in our response.*

Still, when it is happening, we crave certainty. We want simplicity and closure. Some of us get back into the river as if we can return to normalcy — as if our life depended on it.

However, even facing the primal fear of death, the human condition always has held a generative and indefatigable *capacity to reframe.* Even in the gravest of times, even when death is imminent, we are free to choose our attitude, as Viktor Frankl did in WWII concentration camps in *Man's Search for Meaning.*

No matter how daunting the circumstances, how dire the future, how great the loss, we can decide how we will experience life, and yes, even death.

We can reframe a person's demise as a legacy larger than their life. I recall George Floyd's brother, Terrence, at the spot where his brother died.

First of all, first of all...if I'm not over here blowing up stuff, if I'm not over here messing up my community — then what are y'all doing?

Nothing, because that's not going to bring my brother back at all. So, let's do this another way. Let's stop thinking that our voice don't matter and vote…because it's a lot of us and we still going to do this peacefully.

On a much smaller scale, but large in my life, is the fact that my mother died when I was eight years old. Despite the heartbreak, I've since come to realize I owe my sense of independent thinking and self-reliance to her absence. I valued freedom over conformity. (As the years have wised me up, I've come to appreciate the value of interdependence and reliance on others.)

You have survived more than you know. And in the stories of those times is where you find riches to mine to carry the day.

Certain human values and attributes would not exist if not for the worst of days. After all, how else would we know these human capabilities? Empathy, magnanimity, compassion, dignity, nobility, bravery, courage, determination, perseverance, tenacity, fortitude, indefatigability, heroism, ecstatic joy. Grace.

How Do We Stay Connected While Apart?

Surviving as a society right now depends on staying away from each other. Thriving as a society depends on staying close to each other. We are social animals, after all. We must be in community to breed immunity. Isolation breeds depression.

Yet at the very moment in history when we want our immune systems to be the strongest to fight the disease, stress assaults our bodies and psyches — and attacks our immunity. (Moreover, our efforts to right the wrongs of society are also compromised by physical separation.)

We already know how much ongoing negative stress and strain suppresses our immune systems and depresses our moods. We also know that stressors can enhance growth, as long as the strain and struggle are intermittent, as with exercise, for example.

Having *conversations of consequence* can be an antidote to feeling socially distanced and can ward off the risks to mental health that come with isolation. The irony is that even though science says we require human contact, we've come to fear contact with strangers, even family and friends, because it can kill us. It seems to be the *immunity paradox.*

Could connecting in a conversation actually save our lives?

Dan Loritz came to his first Quest retreat 30 years ago at Cambridge University, and now is a senior fellow at the Center for Leadership Philanthropy. Dan told me about a recent visit to his doctor at Mayo Clinic.

"Dan, I'm not concerned about your weight or exercise," his doctor said. "I'm concerned about your having enough social interactions that are really meaningful and engaging." (It sounds as if the doctor is writing a prescription for a walk-and-talk along the river.)

Dan's doctor gave him a chart that shows the benefits of each of many healthy practices. Social engagement was #1, even ahead of stopping smoking. I'd be glad to send the chart to you. It has new meaning in this era.

The entire system of thought you find in these pages and in the book is designed to answer the question of how we can live longer with vitality so we can use our lives to make as great a contribution as possible. On our journey these days, we want to make sure that social distancing is limited only to physical separation and doesn't turn into emotional isolation and loss of engagement with others, or worse.

We are relational beings. This goes right to the point of living longer better.

Social engagement as well as three other active attributes — having purpose, having a positive outlook, and contributing — work synergistically to enliven a person's spirit, and promote health and longevity with vitality. We call them the Quest Quad.

I've already had a longer life than my father and much longer than my mother. In fact, it amazes me: I've lived nearly one-third as long as the U.S. has been a country. How come? I see my lifestyle interventions, especially those four elements, as enough anecdotal evidence, besides the science, to keep me on this path of health and vitality.

Also, in some follow-up writing that's too important to try to squeeze into these few pages, you'll find three frameworks that invite us to a deeper and more intimate conversation: David Cooperrider's appreciative inquiry, the Quest's contribution/philanthropy, and Carol Pearson's heroic journey. In this time of physical separation, these conversations of consequence (at times courageous conversations) can bring closeness, intimacy, and the trust so sorely missing.

These three ways can connect us and get us out of our isolated headspace. Take *contribution,* for example: Jeff Cook, a civic leader in Alaska and beyond, knows how a simple conversation can be a powerful tool in gaining clarity on how we want to contribute — by paying attention to our passion *and* others' passions —

and to "slow the dance down," as he put it. You can hear him in his own words:

Jeff Cook: jimlord.org/bounce-jeff

Can Changing the Conversation Change the Culture (And the World)?

Well-grounded from our time on the riverbank and walking-and-talking along the river, we are now ready to move from awareness to action and get a better bounce to a higher altitude. We can do more than just bounce back to where we were before our current crises. We can all use a good bounce; it's hard to make our best contribution sunk deep in a hole.

For those who want to truly lead in these days in the best way possible, let me come directly to the point: *Changing the world may be as simple as the conversations we convene and the language we use.*

Whether speaking out loud or to yourself, the words you choose shape the world you'll find. "Words create worlds," said Austrian-British philosopher Ludwig Wittgenstein. Change the words you choose and the conversation you convene, and you change the world around you—and that seeds changes in the world at large and even tips the scales of history.

The force of the language is powerful enough a choice that it can begin immediately without adopting an entirely new worldview. Instead of being consumed by deficits, we can move toward a strength-based place to stand. Instead of constant critique, we can move toward appreciation. Instead of a pathological psychology, we can move toward a positive one. We can learn not only from what we choose to see but also from what we choose to overlook. In a word, we can have *choicefulness*.

Language is the rudder of the ship of culture. Case in point: The social chasm made so poignant in Trump's harrowing rise could have been predicted over many years of language of condescension.

Michael Sandel observes:

> Too often in otherwise polite society, elites (progressives emphatically included) unself-consciously belittle working-class whites. We hear talk of 'trailer trash' in 'flyover states' afflicted by 'plumber's butt' — open class insults that pass for wit. This condescension affects political campaigns, as in Hillary Clinton's comment about 'deplorables' and Barack Obama's about people who 'cling to guns or religion.'

New language also infuses the Black Lives Matter and #metoo movements, which are sure to continue as seismic jolts for society. These long-seething inequities have grown ever painfully obvious to so many. The undeniable and long-overdue racial, gender, and class reckoning is the history we're making now, one word at time, one conversation after another.

But isn't *culture* more powerful than words? Indeed, a single word or conversation may seem of little consequence against the force of enormous threats. However, no word or conversation is too small when we look at how habits of thought and talk shape culture. And culture is where you foster the kind of world you want. After all, isn't that what our friendly pilgrims did as they walked and talked together along the river? They created their own culture.

We can see the power of a positive culture in organizational life. For example, when the leaders at Concordia University in Texas wanted to plan for the next decade, they embarked on a "cultural-strengthening" initiative that focused on what they wanted to see in their culture for the future. Cultural norms were given priority over their strategic planning—forecasts that would have been for naught.

Culture leads to the kind of world we want, and organizations are often the vehicle for global social change.

Conversation is the starting point. What we choose to talk about (and what we decide not to hear) invites us into a future that is preferred, possible, and perhaps more within reach than we imagine—a reality that is socially constructed in the conversations we *choose* to convene orally and in the conversational swirl of social media and all.

Now, well-grounded from our time sitting on the riverbank and walking-and-talking along the river, we can move from awareness to action as we use this clarity to get lift.

If we get out of the river and continue the pilgrim's journey, if we have conversations of consequence and see anew all we have to work with, then what is possible for us? Common ground used to be the goal, but if we focus on the individual idiosyncratic talents, desires, and aspirations rather than striving solely for consensus, might we reach higher ground with a wider perspective?

Ask Yourself...
(30-Second Question #2)

What word could you try today that gives you energy rather than taking it?

(For example, how shifting from *safe* to *confident* or *resolved* can move your conversations from commiseration to life-giving?)

Step 3.
Bounce Back Higher

COULD THE LEGACY OF THE PANDEMIC be created in how we grow?

What if there's a silver lining inside the pandemic's existential threat? Suppose instead of merely bouncing back (as comforting as that sounds), or even bouncing back better, what if those who lead were to bounce *higher*? Just like when you're jumping on a trampoline, the harder the downward force, the higher your trajectory.

Could the most significant result of the pandemic be in stretching what it means to be a human being? Could it be that we are now experiencing the expansion of our perspective, our behaviors, and our capabilities to deal with uncertainty and surprises — and at the same time to use that wider view to embolden us toward new horizons and possibilities unimagined until now?

Could the age of the pandemic take you to a height inconceivable until it opened everything to a rethink?

Now is the time — even more than ever before — as counterintuitive as it may feel, to dream and act more boldly. We have people's attention.

A pathogen was our wake up. In the case of climate and the environment, *we* are the pathogen, argues Slovenian philosopher Slavoj Zizek in *Pandemic!* Geologists call our era the Anthropocene Epoch because our human activity has been changing our shared earth so dramatically since 1950, when humans first appeared in the chart of geologic time.

The pandemic could actually end up saving the planet by forcing everyone to take science and our interconnectivity more seriously. Bill Gates, who warned us of pandemic inevitability years before COVID-19, says now that by comparison, ending the pandemic is "very, very easy." Solving climate change, on the other hand, would be "the most amazing thing humanity has ever done."

Rather than the immensity of the problems, we must see the breadth of our capabilities. If we see all we have going for us, all the resources and tailwinds, we stand on firmer ground ready for come-what-may. That is our elasticity: knowing all we have going for us.

Chief among our strengths that will get us through the headwinds and lift us to new heights is our most potent tailwind: our built-in desire to make a difference.

Resilience: Can It Grow?

Yes, to bounce back in trying times, we call on our resilience. But we can do more than rebound. It's better than that.

Recall how bravery, fortitude, and grace would not exist if not for the depths of despair. We surely don't want to live through those depths again or wish them on anyone, but dark days are a prerequisite for wisdom and a full human life.

It's commonly held that facing threats, obstacles and barriers begets resilience. But rather than judging your resilience based on how capable you felt when the pandemic arrived, consider how the challenges you've met since then have strengthened your resilience. Like a muscle, resilience grows when stressed. And the toughest of times don't have to harden us as muscle-bound warriors but can make us more agile, more capable, more human.

When I was an apprentice consultant, my boss told me he had long been in alcoholism recovery. Like him, many whom I've met who've dealt with personal trauma, life-threatening disease, a crisis in aging, or the stigma of differences are among the most human and wise folks I've known. Are depths required to reach the heights?

Exceeding Resilience: Post-Traumatic Growth

If we want to "build back better," to employ Joe Biden's useful term, is there a way to gain even more than *resilience*? After all, to survive a *collective* trauma, we want everything we can get going for us.

If you'd like to believe there's an immense upside to these times, then you'll be as glad as I was to hear about post-traumatic growth. We're not trying to merely restore or *bounce back* to where we were, as great an achievement as that may be for all of us. Rather, we can take advantage of the gift in the meta-disruption to do something better.

Post-traumatic growth (PTG) gives us a way to exceed resilience and break through to a place of greater performance as well as underlying and enduring greater strength and capability—capacities that stand at the ready, come what may. I'm confident you've had this experience in your life. And you've already done more than bounce back, and likely more than once.

PTG is the positive psychological effect that can be experienced after a traumatic event or life crisis. People still suffer. But adversity can expand capabilities and make clearer a person's identity.

A counterpart to post-traumatic stress disorder, PTG was identified in the 1990s by psychologists Richard Tedeschi and Lawrence Calhoun. Their research described the growth that can occur for us:

- We find inner strength to overcome odds that seemed insurmountable.
- We become closer to the people we care about, as well as feeling more compassion for others.
- We more deeply *appreciate* life itself.
- Our relationship to faith and spirituality grows.

From this place of strength, our core values become sturdier, what is essential and what is extravagant becomes clearer, and *who we are* as human beings becomes larger, more visible, and indelible.

All of this growth results in our questioning old assumptions and seeing new possibilities. By interrupting our routine, the trauma and growth open us to changes in understanding ourselves, others, and the world, and sharing with others.

We find this phenomenon described in Nicholas Nassim Taleb's book *Antifragile*, which discusses what happens in surviving a trauma,

> Unlike fragile items, which break when put under stress, antifragile items actually benefit from volatility and shock.
>
> A good example of antifragility is the evolutionary process. It thrives in a volatile environment. With each shock, evolution forces life forms to transform... Shocks and stressors strengthen antifragile systems by forcing them to build up extra capacity.

The best example I've witnessed of going beyond "bounce-back resilience" and experiencing PTG comes from a fourteen-year-old who was being bullied in school. She was sponsored by the school's board chair to come to her first Quest program in Vancouver. Years later, at her second adventure, she confided to Rufus Woods, a newspaper publisher, that she was interested in medical school. He uttered the fateful words, "I know you can do it." Just a few months ago, she was licensed in Canada as Jen Pikard, MD, a board-certified psychiatrist.

Recently, at her fourth retreat in two decades, Dr. Pikard told me that she's discovered a new frontier. When she was asked what challenge she wanted to take on next, I expected she'd say she would be tackling the psychological harm of bullying in schools. However, without hesitation, she replied,

> Stigma. I would most love to go after what I feel is impossible: the intense stigma that healthcare professionals perpetuate to each other about mental and behavioral health. Our patients' worst fears are confirmed when professionals speak with derogatory connotation toward certain diagnoses.

Yes, as if to proclaim that they themselves are not "mentally ill."

When I asked her what would success look like, she answered,

> It would mean a kinder, gentler, more compassionate world. The kinder world I imagined

twenty years ago, when I was first asked as a high school student 'What kind of world do you want?'

Out of her pain, Jen has constructed a valuable contribution—one worthy of who Jen is as a person, and one she can advance via her influence, if not her official role.

In hardship, a person's identity can grow or wither. Personally, I first "stepped out of the river" when I dropped out of high school, just having turned old enough at seventeen to join the Navy. My buddies gave me a six-pack to take on the lonely overnight Greyhound to boot camp. Three months later, my job was to sound taps on my bugle at Navy funerals in New England, a daily exercise to pause and examine the meaning of life and death—an opportunity born of the muted pain of my disrupted home life.

Psychologist and philanthropic leader Molly L. Stranahan was drawn to working with children to reduce suffering; seeing the upside, however, in how it is often from out of our pain that we contribute. You can hear her in her own words:

Molly Stranahan: jimlord.org/bounce-molly

For each of us to make our most significant contribution—perhaps the greatest in our lifetime—we advance our rethink by stepping out of the river to reconsider or redouble our resolve to purpose. And our knowing that we are more capable, thanks to PTG, gives us the oomph to achieve it.

If that contribution is financial or otherwise, put yourself in it—and allow the investment to carry the explicit message you want to send—why you made the commitment. In this way you lead not only in deed, but word as well.

One simple way to make the transition from the pain or doubt to making our contribution can be found in another form of conversation: simply writing a letter. One day long ago, I felt dull and gray as I ended a three-year project to advance a community. So, what to do? I wrote very personal handwritten and heartfelt letters to the two civic leaders I had been working with. As soon as I put down my pen, new energy came to me from praising and honoring them. Strange how that can work, isn't it, growth-promoting for the one who sends and the one who receives?

In these days, a handwritten letter may be more powerful for the recipient than ever before. The intimacy of the personal handwritten letter has actually been shown to make a dramatic difference in suicide prevention. You never know how your smallest action can advance the cause of another person.

Can Our Response to Covid-19 Define This Era?

The pandemic "represents a rare but narrow window of opportunity to reflect, reimagine, and reset our world," writes executive chairman of the World Economic Forum, Klaus Schwab, and Thierry Malleret in *COVID-19: The Great Reset*.

The virus is a wake-up call. It's a wake up to climate and everything being connected in a systemic way, including the certainty of more pandemics because of zoonotics, the transfer of disease from animals to humans.

"We invade the wild, which harbors so many species of animals and plants—and also so many unknown species of viruses and bacteria," writes Heather Quinlan in *Plagues, Pandemics and Viruses*. "We cut down trees, burn jungles, destroy ecosystems, encage animals, and let these viruses loose. When that happens, viruses need a new host. Often, it's us."

While many governments in the West have failed the initial test of this wake-up call, the examples of a different kind of leadership in these pages and in the book offer hope.

"The secret of the West's success over the past four hundred years is its appetite for creative destruction: just when everything looks hopeless, it succeeds in regenerating itself," according to John

Micklethwait, the former editor of *The Economist,* and Adrian Wooldridge, writing in *The Wake-Up Call.* "The question is whether the West can rise to the challenge as it has so many times before and rethink the theory and practice of government — or whether it will fumble about, letting liberty slip away."

In the words of Schwab and Malleret, "In today's world, it is the systemic connectivity between risks, issues, challenges, and also opportunities that matters and determines the future." They go on to give us a summons:

> We are now at a crossroads. One path will take us to a better world: more inclusive, more equitable and more respectful of Mother Nature. The other will take us to a world that resembles the one we just left behind — but worse and constantly dogged by nasty surprises. We must therefore get it right. The looming challenges could be more consequential than we have until now chosen to imagine, but our capacity to reset could also be greater than we had previously dared to hope.

Are we equal to the task? If you've gotten this far with me and you've found some resonance with what I have to say, it seems to me you do have enough of the right stuff. Moreover, given all you've been through, you're more equipped than you were before. So often people fix their gaze on what needs doing, rather than the strengths, resources, capabilities, assets, and blessings — tailwinds all.

While it may seem the first time we've faced such grave universal danger *collectively*, it is worth remembering that in our *personal lives*, long before the specter of the pandemic, we've faced the ultimate risk already: death. You've faced and skirted it, whether you knew it or not. We all have averted the worst of fates.

When I grew up in an apartment building that still stands near Patrick Henry Junior High School in Cleveland's center city, my friend Ralphie, who usually had a runny nose, lived nearby. When the two of us were about five years old, and the windows of our homes were open one summer day, I wandered out of a window onto the black iron fire escape three stories up. My leg got stuck. As my father tried to free it, little Ralphie was on the ground talking to me, calming me. "If not for Ralphie, I don't think you would have lived," my father told me.

Who knows what close calls we've survived? The near miss on the highway ... the fire ... the asymptomatic carrier of coronavirus?

We have already been tested and passed trials we weren't even aware of, have forgotten or overlooked. We have weathered storms. We're now more capable for it. What does that awareness do to our outlook, our frame of reference, our sense of self and identity?

Ask Yourself...
(30-Second Question #3)

What is one capability you have discovered in yourself since the pandemic began? And standing in that strength, what is one thing you can say or do today that is important to you?

"(Perhaps you've overlooked that ability, undervalued it, taken it for granted, or simply denied it.)

Who Will Lead?

ONCE WE'VE GOTTEN OUT OF THE RIVER and taken a walk along the riverbank, we've grounded ourselves in enough awareness so we can bounce higher. The French say, "reculer pour mieux sauter." Draw back the better to leap. A strategic withdrawal from the setback allows us to advance further. Be it a midlife crisis, a nervous breakdown or getting out of the turbulent flow, we come out the better for it, even if at times it is only a brief meditation or even just a deep breath.

Now it's time to return to the river, and act in a new and refreshed way.

We've grown from our solitary time to our solidarity — from *me* courage to *we* citizenry.

To make our response greater than disease and the upheaval, what can we call on?

We Can Elicit Each Other's Hidden Resources to Create a Citizenry of *We*

Does this difficult time offer us a unique opportunity to make a unique contribution? What more might we be able to do together if we attend to our individual capacity, our presence, our equanimity? And allow that to show up in fresh and inspiring ways?

Gary Hubbell, consultant in the Quest, observes:

Now is the time to inspire everyone around us to rethink and intensify their unique contribution—one only *they* can make. As we reflect, we deepen our awareness. The gravitational pull—from within and without—is really a *choice* about our own response. By choosing to be inspired by this moment, we propel ourselves toward possibility, always there but previously unseen.

Gary Hubbell: jimlord.org/bounce-gary

Who's Leading Us?

As we emerge from this time of converging crises, one question will echo for decades if not centuries: *Where was our leadership?* Undoubtedly the people who could have led us have failed us. But what if there is a deeper, truer kind of leadership right under our noses — or facing us in the mirror?

May the answer be that the capacity to influence our shared destiny was within us all along? It just took a cataclysmic crisis to activate our latent power? The monarch never starts the revolution.

Any positive revolution is going to start with *the people* – those who have the ability, will, and courage to use their influence (more than they know they have), and many more who have felt powerless until hearing the call in these peculiar days.

Imagine if all the people who want to change the world *knew* they could.

I want to shake so many shoulders so they can see our self-efficacy and own up to what we've already done — which is key to understanding what more we can do. And then I want to shake all of the shoulders collectively because if we each reach new heights, and we do it together, what could be possible?

Especially when we consider that the world has not had access to all of its talent, not by a long shot. Until recently, more than half of our population — women as well as Black, indigenous, and people of color (BIPOC)—haven't even been on the roster for roles in leadership.

Now we watch in amazement as women, who make up only ten percent of the chiefs of state in the world, stand out for how much more effectively they've handled the COVID-19 crisis than their male counterparts. Leading the way have been Tsai Ingwen, the first woman president of Taiwan; Jacinda Ardern, the iconoclastic prime minister of New Zealand; and Europe's bulwark, Angela Merkel, all of them contrasts to their cavalier and machismo counterparts. I'm curious to see the long-term consequences of Kamala Harris' ascent and Amanda Gorman's poetry.

If we want to handle whatever is thrown to us, why would we leave most of the world's team, many of whom are more humane than the former players, on the bench? And not just people already in power, but all of us, no matter how much position or influence we may have in the world, or not. This is both a global opportunity and a deeply personal one for each of us.

My greatest inspiration comes when we find people like my friend Anita Johnson, a young Black leader who works each day to get people of color into careers in medicine, from high school students to top administrative and academic posts. Says Anita, "It took my realizing that I *do belong*—that I am a worthy member of society—to inspire others to believe that about themselves." Here you can listen to her insights:

Anita Johnson: jimlord.org/bounce-anita

We also have waiting in the wings, the kind of young people Anita works with—the iGen folks, born 1995-2012, who are different from most of today's society in how strongly they seek a more humane and responsible society. Or perhaps they're not waiting but already acting?

Most of us know the first name of Greta Thunberg, the 16-year-old girl who unflinchingly and fiercely rang the bell for planetary health when she spoke at the United Nations and was pictured on the cover of *Time* magazine.

At the same time, the power of *informal influence* has risen, giving us yet another source of leadership. Such influence lies beyond the power inherent in a leader's formal role; it exists in their very presence as they use the Gestalt principle of *self as instrument*. The power of informal influence is also possessed by those who claim their outsider's voice, like the Parkland shooting survivors.

Joining the chorus of power to the people, many organizations are becoming more egalitarian.

Stakeholder capitalism, employee activism and ownership, corporate social responsibility, sustainability — all point to the belief: for everyone to thrive, the pie must grow for all. It's the right thing to do, and we're seeing that inclusive capitalism is where to find the rewards for the enterprise, as well as everyone else. It all starts with recognizing that every person yearns to contribute. As much as what you get, the pie includes what you want to give, as we'll soon see with *contributive* justice.

Our innate desire to contribute is too often thwarted by leaders who think that people must be motivated, coaxed, and incentivized, even as such interventions steamroll over their existing urge to make a difference.

We also find this directive and controlling spirit in work typically called *fundraising*. The word itself focuses on the organization's needs while *philanthropy* is about the desires of the donor, waiting to find vehicles for expression.

"I am convinced that far more idealistic aspiration exists than is ever evident. Just as the rivers we see are much less numerous than the underground streams, so the idealism that is visible is minor compared to what men and women carry in their hearts, unreleased or scarcely released," said Nobel Prize-winning humanitarian Albert Schweitzer. "Mankind is waiting and longing for those who can accomplish the task of untying what is knotted and bringing the underground waters to the surface."

Whether for small leadership or large, opportunity abounds in a time like this one. Nancy Koehn, business historian at Harvard Business School, has studied courageous crisis leaders for two decades and says that "Through this work I know that real leaders are not born; the ability to help others triumph over adversity is not written into their genetic code. They are, instead, made. They are forged in crisis."

In work settings we can remind people why their work matters, and the key role that each person plays, she says. "We now have a powerful opportunity for organizations and teams of all kinds to better understand their strengths." We can see more clearly now what really engages and motivates people.

You are stronger than you know, and a crisis is the only way to find out. We can work across boundaries we've created for ourselves in realizing this universal abiding craving to make a difference.

Creating
Contributive Justice

"Any hope of renewing our moral and civic life depends on understanding how, over the past four decades, our social bonds and respect for one another came unraveled," writes Michael Sandel in *The Tyranny of Merit*. Politicians have been missing something, he says.

> They have been offering working-class and middle-class voters a greater measure of *distributive justice*—fairer, fuller access to the fruits of economic growth. But what these voters want even more is a greater measure of *contributive justice*—an opportunity to win the social recognition and esteem that goes with producing what others need and value.

> When we say distributive justice, often called *social justice*, we're talking about the fairness of what people get. Contributive justice is the opposite: it's what people give, what they contribute to society.

> "Theories of contributive justice," says Sandel, "teach us that we are most fully human when we contribute to the common good and earn the esteem of our fellow citizens for the contributions we make."

But now, ever-greater conflict and contention have been estranging us from understanding and appreciating each other.

One everyday example is how someone with a bare face and without a shot in the arm has become a symbol of strength among those who put personal freedom before collective safety. It takes all the compassion and empathy I can muster to try to understand that which I scorn. I have to remind myself that shaming alienates, while connecting has a better chance of influencing behavior. Instead of finger-pointing, I admit that I too don't like wearing a mask or getting a shot.

On these pages, we've tried to understand what motivates prosocial behavior. That understanding can be furthered by grasping what motivates the "anti's" — the anti-mask wearers and anti-vaxxers — to resist our new shared reality.

Fear is operating here, some folks scared out of their wits. I used to think populism was fear of change, and then I thought, ah-ha, it is also classism, and now I also see *credentialism*. At the root of much of the divided society we see is the insidious disdain for the less educated.

"By 2016, many working people chafed at the sense that well-schooled elites looked down on them with condescension," says Sandel, as reported in *The New York Times*. "At a time when racism and sexism are out of favor (discredited though not eliminated), credentialism is the last acceptable prejudice."

Strong is the implication that it's become a contest of the smart vs. the dumb, with each side knowing which is their team. One side's affliction is humiliation; the other side's, hubris.

The disdain goes both ways: the uncredentialed scorn the intellectuals, as a battle rages against "elitist" science.

For a long time, I tried to understand one of the other *isms* at the core of discord — racism. I was leading workshops in South Africa at the time when swimming pools were first integrated. What I'm about to say may sound insensitive today, given the profound pain inflicted by white supremacists. But I feel it makes an important point for our current era, especially after the deadly insurrection on the U.S. Capitol.

As I worked with some of the fine folks at the Afrikaans-language University of the Orange Free State, I tried to grasp what it was like for them as the white minority. They felt so threatened and afraid *their* identity would be snuffed out by people who seemed so different from them, that they believed separation of the races — apartheid — was the only answer.

Yet despite the cost of those fears to the majority population of Black South Africans who lived under that oppression, they showed their spirit of forgiveness amidst accountability. Wow! They were so non-retributive and bold that when they finally won their rights to their nation, they established the Truth and Reconciliation Commission to make peace — and gave an enduring lesson to us all.

We are also being awakened to *casteism* by writer Isabel Wilkerson, author of *Caste: The Origin of Our Discontents*, not just in India but in the U.S. and elsewhere. One of the facilitators of the Quest retreat from India, Vibha uses only her first name so she might be known as a person rather than by her caste.

Since the onset of the pandemic, 18,000 people have benefited from Vibha's "Corona, Gratitude and Physical Distancing" live online workshops designed to mitigate the emotional and mental health risks of these times — offered without a formal fee but for which participants pay what they choose, in a "currency of trust."

Classism, credentialism, casteism, and more. Stigmatizing trumps humanizing. Tribe and herd wins over humanity. Where does discord and hatred actually come from?

I found an insight that intrigued me from an evolutionary anthropologist, Brian Hare at Duke University, and his wife, research scientist Vanessa Woods. It's a tall leap from humanity, but points toward a worthwhile insight for me: Among animals, we find aggressive chimpanzees north of the Congo River and more peaceful bonobos south of the river. How is it that these two species that appear identical are so different in behavior? In a word, *resources*. Chimpanzees live where food is scarcer. Bonobos live where they don't have to worry as much about food or compete for resources.

On a human level, acknowledging how much we have going for us, even when things seem to have gone badly, can be a strategy to alleviate conflict and lift health and vitality.

It's said that among members of the Babemba tribe, when someone acts outside of the norms, instead of punishment, they are met with praise for their human qualities. A group surrounds the person and shouts out attributes they admire about the person. Imagine the effect if you were in the center of that circle, expecting to be chastised.

When people who are stressed are reminded of what they have going for them — their resources — they stand in that power capable of more than they would be had they been beaten down.

Might that be the path to avoiding the worst of collective fates, even a new kind of Civil War, if each of us can simply feel more worthy? And might it fall to those who are psychosocially mature to find ways to appreciate those of extreme difference — something of value worth noting in the other human being, just as we wish they would see in us?

When we feel full and well-grounded, we can take on anything.

Are Resources the Key?

Is hate what happens to people when they feel depleted, instead of feeling safe and worthy, recognized for their strengths and capabilities? It may be less about how much we actually *have* as it is about how much we *believe* we have and how resourceful we feel. We can live in contrast to the sense of helplessness and hopelessness that Martin Seligman articulates via his work in the growing field of positive psychology.

We can also find out which strengths can best define our futures through Tom Rath's contribution of *StrengthsFinder*.

Developing the skill to see strengths and assets — recognizing our life-giving forces — is also the foundation of David Cooperrider's appreciative inquiry, the greatest theoretical contribution to my life and which you'll find at the heart of *What Kind of World Do You Want?*

David would say that when our gaze moves up from the self to society, we find the same principle operating: regardless of how much we have, when we *feel* resource-laden (personally and in our group and community), we feel stronger, more capable, with more health and vitality. And we are prepared for a more significant contribution to benefit the common good — greater social impact.

This worldview that I try to live was fortified when I looked at the relationship between resources that are shared, plentiful or not, and the illness of depression. Although we understand today there is more than one source of depression, a recent study suggests that when humans feel resources are sufficient and shared, they are more likely to avoid depression. The Hadza tribe in Tanzania shows no signs of the disease.

Cultural psychologist, Coren Apicella noted, "Nearly one-hundred percent of the resources that enter the tribe are redistributed ... a high degree of equality. Egalitarian societies are free of depression." Apicella reports a tribesman saying, "No matter how hungry we are, we always share whatever animals we caught."

Around me and in me, I see it time and again, when we human beings feel more abundance than scarcity, we become more cooperative than competitive, and kinder and more generous. Even with ourselves. The more secure we feel, taking stock of what we have, rather than fixating on what we lack, the more confident we are, the more energy and staying power we possess, the more we are catapulted to undertake what was unimaginable until now.

Of course, in today's world, paying attention to what we have and what we've achieved can feel counterproductive, like "letting up the pressure," slipping into complacency and losing the momentum. But we've found quite the opposite. Believing that we have more resources than it seems, and we are more resourceful than we feel—even if too rosy a calculation—serves us best. Such a sense of personal power paves the way for our boldest answer to the virus and the accompanying swirl of opportunities disguised as problems.

You are abundant with resources. You've opened your eyes to them, preserved and augmented them on the riverbank. You've explored your possibilities on a journey of heroic proportion. No matter the profound challenges of our time, you've seen how you can rise to them, reframe them as possibilities, and bounce back higher, with greater perspective and vision. Your greatest contribution is yet to come.

You were made for this moment.

Ask Yourself...
(Bonus Question — The Biggest One)

I've imagined our walk as more of a conversation than a monologue. How about if you now have a conversation with someone else about these ideas, as if you are both strolling by the riverside?

Here's a question you can start with,

"Look back to 2020. In all the ups and downs, what do you see that was a high point for you since the lockdown? Let's go back to that moment as if you have a video camera and tell me what you see and what you hear. Tell me the story."

Keep the spotlight on them as if you're interviewing them, rather than a back-and-forth. After they finish their story, you can turn the spotlight to tell your story.

After that conversation with one person, you might gather a small circle of people to talk about the ideas here. How are you seeing those ideas play out around you?

Watch how the conversation changes when you use a positive and life-giving frame (as appreciative inquiry suggests).

A simple conversation like this between two or more could inspire (breathe life into) y'all.

Or if you'd rather take a smaller step, you could now do just one simple thing: Take a breath, a deep one. (I just did.)

Be in Touch with Me

WHETHER THIS BOOK HAS BEEN A GIFT TO YOURSELF or a gift from someone else, I hope it has inspired and lifted up your basic human spirit—that rising spirit of the people found in the stories and videos in this book. So please accept this gift in recognition of the kind of person you've shown yourself to be — *someone whose presence on this planet has made a difference.* Are you ready to begin to own up to that yet? I hope so!

If you happen to have gifted this book to yourself, congratulations. You've stayed with me this far and that says a lot to me about the kind of person you are. I want to fortify your confidence to be an inspiration to others.

———

I would love to hear from you. Your words could influence what I write in the future, making this monologue more of a conversation. Maybe you'll tell me a story sparked by what you've read here. I'd like that.

Here's the email address: quest@jimlord.org. You are likely to get a reply from me or one of our circle members.

I'm now writing about the eight daily practices I'm using for optimal health, especially mental health, during this epic time. I'll be glad to send that to you.

If you'd like to get to know some of the folks that you met in these pages, and see them speaking in their own words—for example, Kim Scott, talking about the three questions on mental health—please visit the website of the Center for Leadership Philanthropy: jimlord.org/retreats.

About Jim Lord

Jim Lord is the author of the classic book for board members, *The Raising of Money*, considered a foundational contribution to philanthropy. It has been the bestselling book on the topic, having reached more than 250,000 readers. His work with philanthropists, leaders, and their causes has helped nonprofits to raise billions and taught him more about what motivates people than any book, course, or expert. That's the wisdom he shares in his writing and retreats.

Jim has spent fifty years effectively answering the deceptively simple question he asked on his first day as the youngest consultant with the oldest capital campaign firm: "Why do people give away their money?"

Answering that question has turned into a life's work that has taken him from consulting with small-

town YWCAs to the Vatican and the White House —
and it has brought civic leaders and university
presidents to his Quest strategic retreats.

In the years since publishing *The Raising of Money*,
he has developed the Quest strategic retreats for leaders
and philanthropists to envision the kind of world they
want and their role in flourishing it, including what
he calls their "Next" — their next big idea. People from
fifty countries have attended, many several times —
and a growing cadre of alums have been certified to
facilitate the program.

Jim withdrew from speaking to continue his
research and work with global thought leaders on the
most current ideas in social psychology, organizational
behavior, community development, and global social
change — and to refine his model of prosocial behavior
based on that original question of why we give.

Jim's second major book, *What Kind of World Do
You Want?*, was written after 9/11 for civic leaders and
socially engaged individuals to show how people have
reframed problems into possibilities. It lays out how
rethinking our capacities can lead us to the greatest
contributions of our lives.

Now *Bounce Back Higher*, a manifesto and companion
for our times, serves as a prequel and new introduction
to *What Kind of World Do You Want?*

With a grounded, heartfelt, and inspiring message
that our biggest contribution is ahead of us, it shares
three steps to: clear our minds, take a walk-and-talk,
and elevate higher than ever before — all so we can

make the most significant contribution of our lives, and lift people with inspiring confidence.

Most of all, it's a call to action to shape a post-pandemic world that is better than we can imagine.

These epic times offer us a moment like none before to discover our ultimate personal answer to the question of why we give.

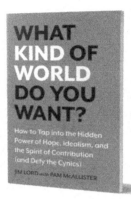

Further Reading – a Gift

To continue the conversation, you can claim a complimentary audio and electronic copy of the book mentioned on these pages, *What Kind of World Do You Want?* The pages you are reading now are, in a sense, a new introduction to that book, published after 9/11, another traumatic time.

The book was originally distributed privately by the Center for Leadership Philanthropy and is now publicly available.

There is also a course related to the book as well as a strategic retreat, which is now being offered by a cadre of retreat alums.

To download your copy of the book, please visit: jimlord.org/what-kind-of-world.

Quest Strategic Retreats

When you become a force for grounded hope and inspired action, anything is possible. Imagine. What if you could inspire everyone around you to make their greatest contribution—the one that they're longing to make?

Find out more about the Quest Strategic Retreat (offered as a virtual retreat or an in-person live event) and how to apply at jimlord.org/retreats, and the by-invitation Facilitator Certification Program at jimlord.org/certification.

NOTES

NOTES

NOTES